FIND CHAFFY NOW

by Jamie Smart

SCHOLASTIC

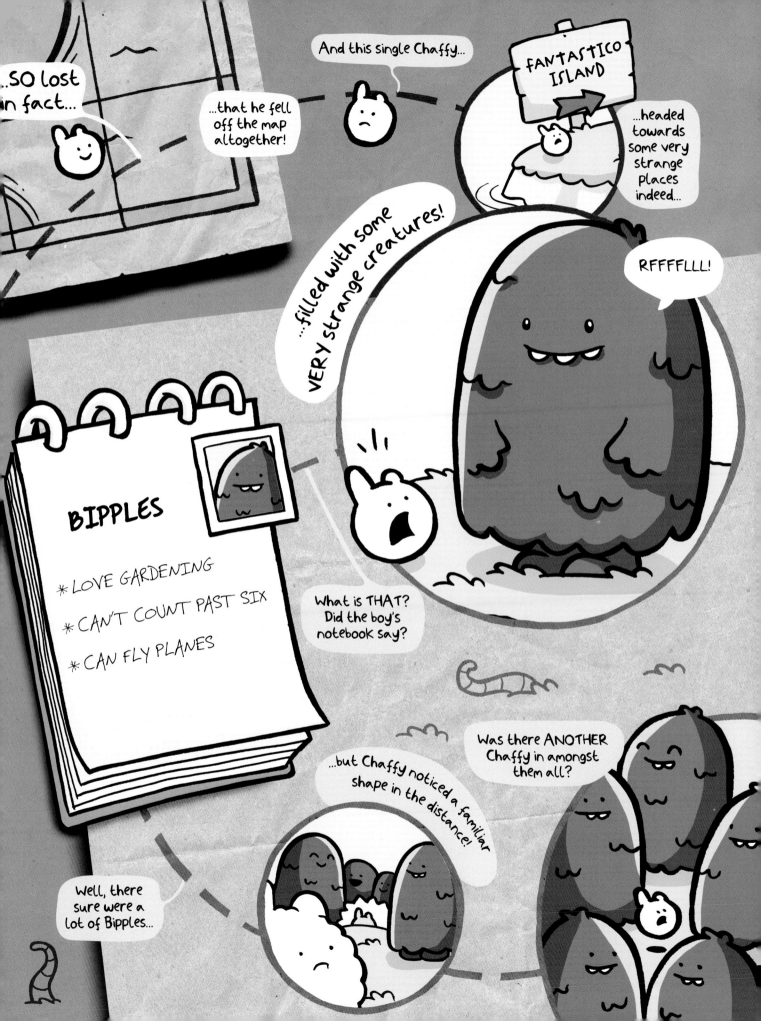

LOST

2 Chaffies to find!
(But one looks a little different...)

...when suddenly, a very weird creature lurched towards them!

GRAWRRR!

SKELLINGTUNS

* LOVE FIGHTING (EACH OTHER, MAINLY)

* TERRIFIED OF SNEEZING

* SLEEP UNDERGROUND!

Quickly, check what it is!

Could they make it through the Skellingtuns to find him?

The Chaffies were a little scared, until they saw the shape of ANOTHER Chaffy!

~ THE BATTLE OF THE SCARY ~
# SKELLINGTUNS!

LOST

3 Chaffies to find!
(But one looks a little different...)

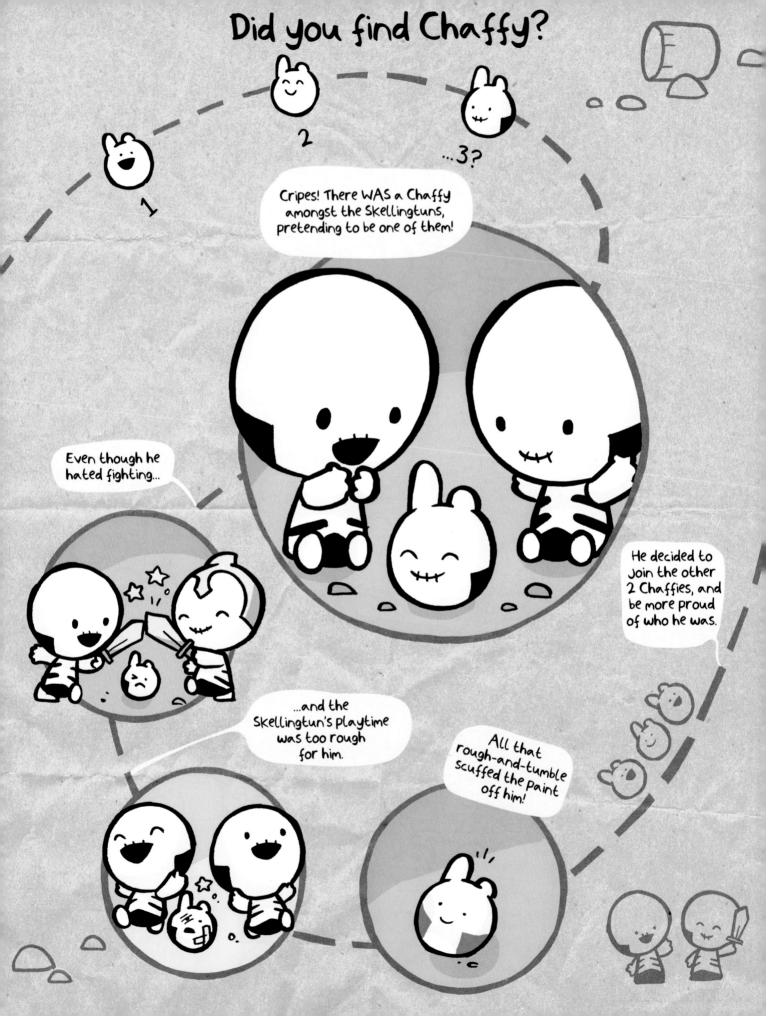

3 Chaffies travelled together through this strange land...
...until they found themselves in an underwater cavern, with a very unhappy looking thing!
BUHHHHH!
GLUMBOS
* MISERABLE SEA CREATURES
* VERY GRUMPY
* HAVE INVERTED BOTTOMS! (HUH?)
Goodness, what's bothering HIM?
If they could get through the Glumbos, maybe they could find him!
But wait, ANOTHER Chaffy? Down here?
Wow, an inverted bottom would make anyone grumpy!

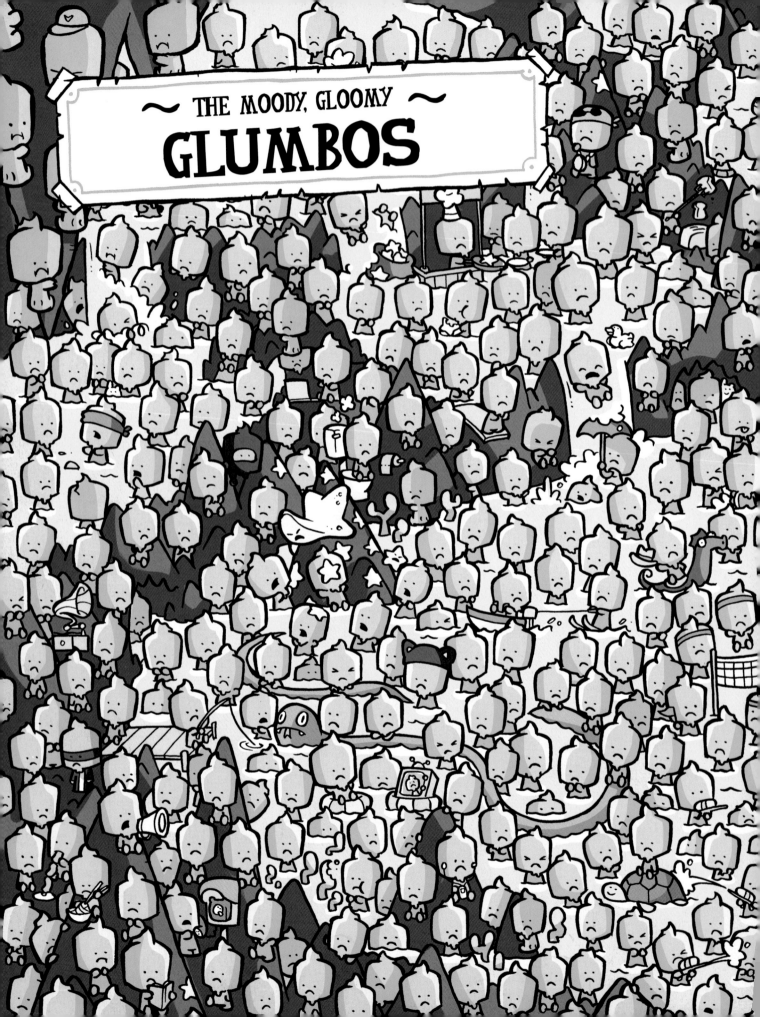

~ THE MOODY, GLOOMY ~
# GLUMBOS

LOST

4 Chaffies to find!
(But one looks a little different...)

LOST

5 Chaffies to find! (But one looks a little different...)

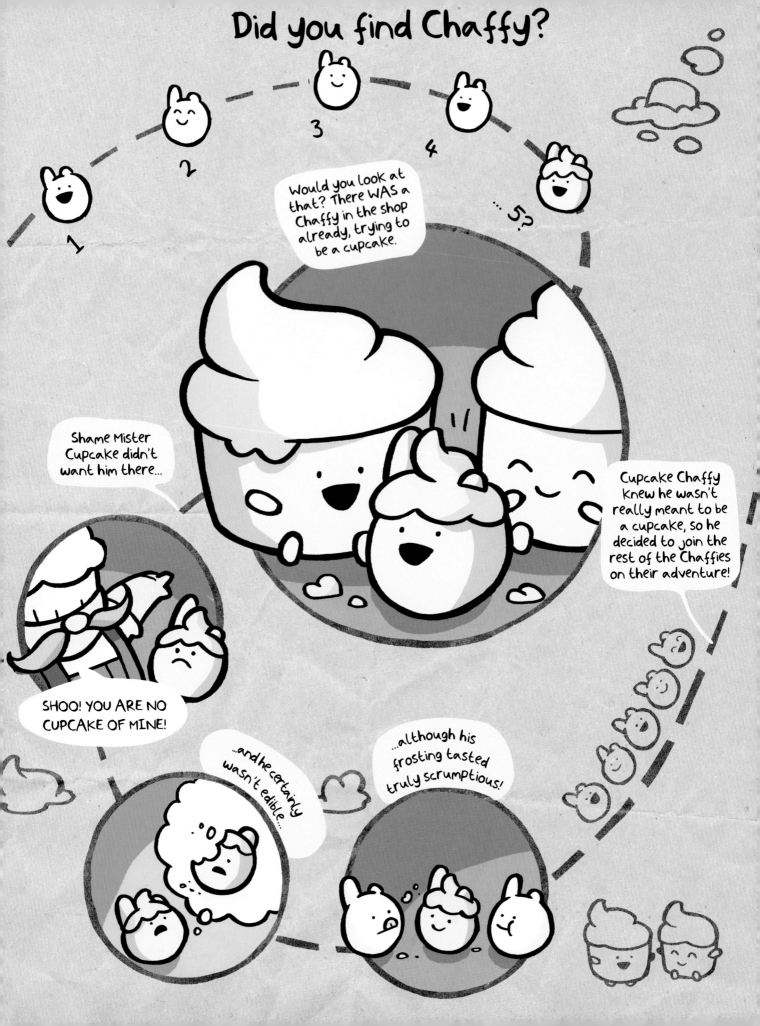

LOST

6 Chaffies to find!
(But one looks a little different...)

...as the weather started to get a lot colder...

...some creatures, that looked like PENGUINS, came out to say hello.

BZZZ FFT!

SPACE PENGUINS

* SCARED OF THE COLOUR ORANGE

* ALLERGIC TO PUPPIES AND WITCHES

* CRASH-LANDED FROM THE PLANET HUFFHUFF

BZZZ FFT? That didn't sound like penguin language!

...was there a Chaffy here already?

Hmm, maybe these weren't the first Chaffies to meet Space Penguins...

LOST

9 Chaffies to find!
(But one looks a little different...)

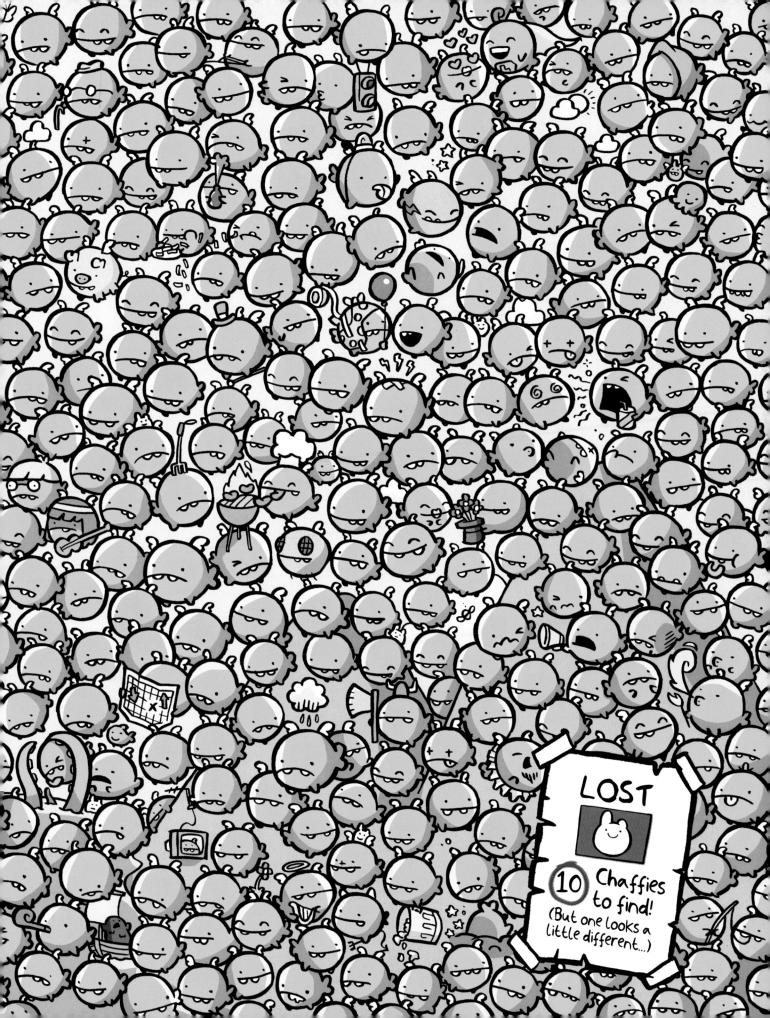

LOST

10 Chaffies to find! (But one looks a little different...)

~ THE LAND OF THE ~
# GIANT CHAFFIES

LOST

11 Chaffies to find!

← This size.

WHAT ELSE DID YOU FIND?

What a journey we've had, following these Chaffies on their weirdly wonderful adventure on Fantastico Island! But for all the Bipples, Skellingtuns, Glumbos, Living Cupcakes, Hot Plops, Cold Plops, Schnoodges, Space Penguins, Bumbleclumps, Lurrrrps and Giant Chaffies we've encountered, there were a vast array of randomly ludicrous things to be found along the way.

Were you sharp-witted enough to spot THESE sights?

A Police Cupcake

A rockabilly Cupcake

A baby Cupcake

An arty Bipple

A Bipple catching butterflies

A Bipple dressed like a dinosaur!

A Skellingtun dressed like a bird

A Skellingtun dressed like a swimmer

A Glumbo riding a turtle

A birthday Glumbo

A sledging Skellingtun

A Glumbo playing hide-and-seek

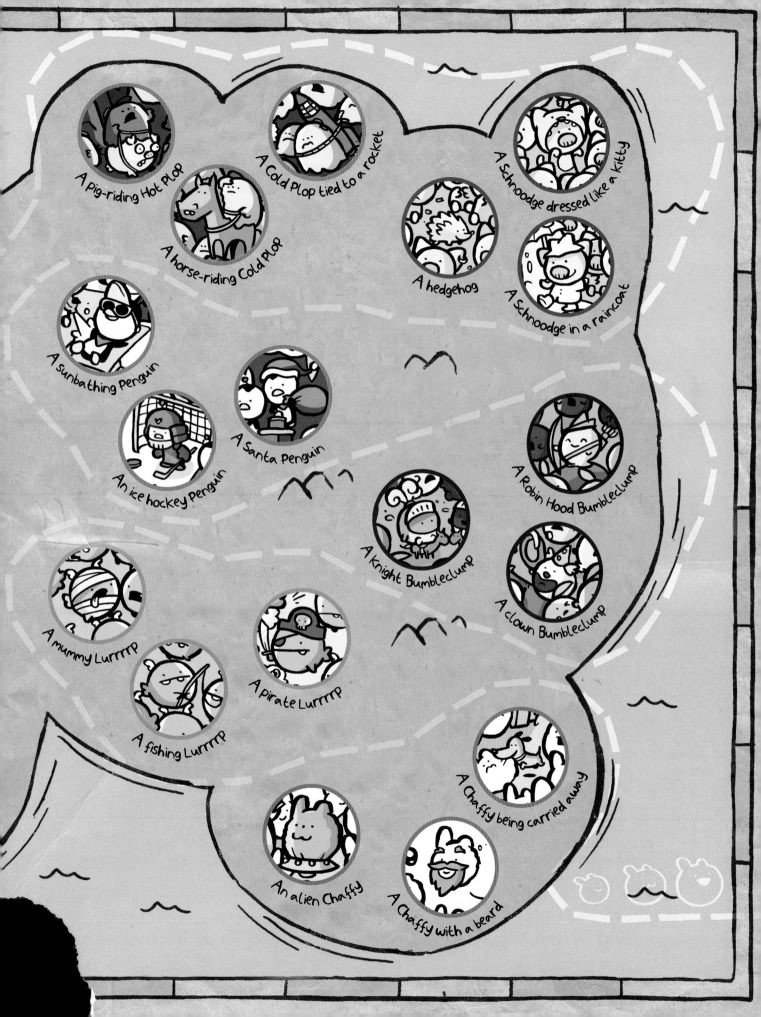

You did it! You found Chaffy!

In fact, you found LOADS of them, and helped bring them all home!

The search isn't over yet, though. There are still countless Chaffies out there in the world, all looking for somewhere to call home.

They've been to some extraordinary places already, but who KNOWS where they'll end up next.
If you're very lucky, you might even find one! Here are some good places to look...

In a bowl of custard!

Underneath a pillow!

In the sky!

On top of a monkey, on top of a mountain!

And be sure to tell us you found one, at

www.findchaffy.co.uk